# 50 Kid-Friendly Meals for Large Families

By: Kelly Johnson

# Table of Contents

- Taco Bar Night
- Spaghetti and Meatballs
- Homemade Chicken Nuggets
- Mini Pizzas with Assorted Toppings
- Macaroni and Cheese Bake
- Sloppy Joes
- Baked Ziti with Mozzarella
- Chicken Fajitas
- Vegetable Stir-Fry with Rice
- Cheesy Broccoli and Rice Casserole
- Quesadilla Platter
- Beef and Bean Chili
- Stuffed Bell Peppers
- Pasta Primavera
- Crispy Fish Tacos
- Homemade Lasagna
- Grilled Cheese and Tomato Soup
- Baked Chicken Drumsticks
- Vegetable Fried Rice
- BBQ Pulled Pork Sandwiches
- Stuffed Shells with Ricotta
- Coconut Curry Chicken
- Tortilla Wraps with Assorted Fillings
- Sweet and Sour Chicken
- Shepherd's Pie
- Breakfast-for-Dinner: Pancakes and Sausages
- Beef Tacos with All the Fixings
- Creamy Tomato Pasta
- Mini Meatloaves
- Chili Cheese Dogs
- Potato and Cheese Pierogi
- Vegetable Soup with Grilled Cheese
- Pulled BBQ Chicken Tacos
- Fish Sticks with Dipping Sauces
- Pasta with Alfredo Sauce
- Chicken and Rice Casserole

- Baked Potato Bar
- Pasta Salad with Veggies and Dressing
- Chicken Enchiladas
- Tater Tot Casserole
- Homemade Empanadas
- Rice and Bean Burritos
- Fried Rice with Chicken and Peas
- Minestrone Soup
- Teriyaki Chicken with Steamed Broccoli
- Egg and Cheese Breakfast Burritos
- Cheesy Taco Pasta
- Spinach and Cheese Stuffed Shells
- Beef and Broccoli Stir-Fry
- Crispy Potato Wedges with Dips

## Taco Bar Night

### Ingredients

- Taco shells (soft and hard)
- Seasoned ground beef or shredded chicken
- Toppings: shredded lettuce, diced tomatoes, chopped onions, jalapeños, guacamole, sour cream, shredded cheese, and salsa

### Instructions

1. Prepare the seasoned meat in a skillet over medium heat until cooked through.
2. Set up a taco bar with taco shells and all the toppings in separate bowls.
3. Allow everyone to build their own tacos with their favorite ingredients.

## Spaghetti and Meatballs

## Ingredients

- 1 pound spaghetti
- 1 pound ground beef or turkey
- 1 egg
- 1/2 cup breadcrumbs
- 1/4 cup grated Parmesan cheese
- 1 jar marinara sauce
- Salt and pepper to taste
- Fresh basil for garnish

## Instructions

1. Cook spaghetti according to package instructions.
2. In a bowl, combine ground meat, egg, breadcrumbs, Parmesan, salt, and pepper. Form into meatballs.
3. Cook meatballs in a skillet until browned, then add marinara sauce and simmer.
4. Serve meatballs over spaghetti and garnish with fresh basil.

# Homemade Chicken Nuggets

## Ingredients

- 1 pound chicken breasts, cut into bite-sized pieces
- 1 cup flour
- 2 eggs, beaten
- 2 cups breadcrumbs
- Salt and pepper to taste
- Cooking oil for frying

## Instructions

1. Preheat oil in a deep fryer or large skillet over medium heat.
2. Season chicken pieces with salt and pepper. Dredge in flour, dip in eggs, then coat with breadcrumbs.
3. Fry nuggets until golden brown and cooked through. Drain on paper towels and serve with dipping sauces.

# Mini Pizzas with Assorted Toppings

## Ingredients

- 1 package pizza dough or pre-made pizza crusts
- Pizza sauce
- Shredded mozzarella cheese
- Assorted toppings: pepperoni, bell peppers, olives, mushrooms, onions, etc.

## Instructions

1. Preheat the oven according to the pizza dough instructions.
2. Roll out dough and cut into small rounds or squares.
3. Spread sauce, add cheese, and top with assorted toppings.
4. Bake until the crust is golden and the cheese is melted.

## Macaroni and Cheese Bake

### Ingredients

- 1 pound elbow macaroni
- 4 cups shredded cheese (cheddar, mozzarella, or a blend)
- 2 cups milk
- 1/4 cup butter
- 1/4 cup flour
- Salt and pepper to taste
- 1 cup breadcrumbs (for topping)

### Instructions

1. Preheat oven to 350°F (175°C). Cook macaroni according to package directions.
2. In a saucepan, melt butter, whisk in flour, and gradually add milk until thickened. Stir in cheese until melted.
3. Combine macaroni with cheese sauce, season with salt and pepper, and transfer to a baking dish. Top with breadcrumbs.
4. Bake for 20-25 minutes until bubbly and golden.

**Sloppy Joes**

## Ingredients

- 1 pound ground beef or turkey
- 1 cup ketchup
- 1 tablespoon Worcestershire sauce
- 1 tablespoon mustard
- Salt and pepper to taste
- Hamburger buns

## Instructions

1. In a skillet, cook ground meat over medium heat until browned. Drain excess fat.
2. Stir in ketchup, Worcestershire sauce, mustard, salt, and pepper. Simmer for 10 minutes.
3. Serve mixture on hamburger buns.

## Baked Ziti with Mozzarella

### Ingredients

- 1 pound ziti pasta
- 2 cups marinara sauce
- 2 cups ricotta cheese
- 2 cups shredded mozzarella cheese
- 1/2 cup grated Parmesan cheese
- Fresh basil for garnish

### Instructions

1. Preheat oven to 375°F (190°C). Cook ziti according to package directions.
2. In a large bowl, mix cooked pasta with marinara sauce and ricotta cheese.
3. Transfer to a baking dish and top with mozzarella and Parmesan cheese.
4. Bake for 25-30 minutes until bubbly. Garnish with basil before serving.

# Chicken Fajitas

## Ingredients

- 1 pound chicken breasts, sliced
- 1 bell pepper, sliced
- 1 onion, sliced
- 2 tablespoons fajita seasoning
- Tortillas
- Toppings: sour cream, guacamole, salsa, shredded cheese

## Instructions

1. In a skillet, cook chicken, bell peppers, and onion over medium heat until chicken is cooked through.
2. Stir in fajita seasoning and cook for an additional 2-3 minutes.
3. Serve mixture in tortillas with desired toppings.

# Vegetable Stir-Fry with Rice

## Ingredients

- 2 cups mixed vegetables (bell peppers, broccoli, carrots, snap peas)
- 2 tablespoons soy sauce
- 1 tablespoon sesame oil
- 2 cloves garlic, minced
- 1 inch ginger, minced
- 2 cups cooked rice
- Green onions for garnish

## Instructions

1. Heat sesame oil in a large skillet over medium-high heat. Add garlic and ginger, sauté for 1 minute.
2. Add mixed vegetables and stir-fry until tender-crisp, about 5-7 minutes.
3. Stir in soy sauce and cooked rice, mixing well. Cook for an additional 2-3 minutes.
4. Serve hot, garnished with chopped green onions.

# Cheesy Broccoli and Rice Casserole

## Ingredients

- 2 cups cooked rice
- 2 cups broccoli florets, steamed
- 1 can cream of mushroom soup
- 1 cup shredded cheddar cheese
- 1/2 cup milk
- Salt and pepper to taste
- 1/2 cup breadcrumbs (optional for topping)

## Instructions

1. Preheat the oven to 350°F (175°C).
2. In a large bowl, combine cooked rice, steamed broccoli, cream of mushroom soup, cheddar cheese, milk, salt, and pepper.
3. Pour mixture into a greased baking dish. If using, sprinkle breadcrumbs on top.
4. Bake for 25-30 minutes until bubbly and golden.

## Quesadilla Platter

## Ingredients

- 4 large flour tortillas
- 2 cups shredded cheese (cheddar, Monterey Jack, or a blend)
- Assorted fillings: cooked chicken, beans, peppers, onions
- Salsa and sour cream for serving

## Instructions

1. Heat a skillet over medium heat. Place a tortilla in the skillet and sprinkle half with cheese and desired fillings.
2. Fold the tortilla in half and cook until golden brown, about 2-3 minutes per side. Repeat with remaining tortillas.
3. Cut quesadillas into wedges and serve with salsa and sour cream.

## Beef and Bean Chili

### Ingredients

- 1 pound ground beef
- 1 can kidney beans, drained and rinsed
- 1 can diced tomatoes
- 1 onion, chopped
- 2 cloves garlic, minced
- 2 tablespoons chili powder
- Salt and pepper to taste

### Instructions

1. In a large pot, brown the ground beef over medium heat. Drain excess fat.
2. Add onion and garlic, cooking until softened. Stir in chili powder, salt, and pepper.
3. Add kidney beans and diced tomatoes, simmer for 20-30 minutes.
4. Serve hot, garnished with cheese or sour cream if desired.

## Stuffed Bell Peppers

### Ingredients

- 4 bell peppers, tops removed and seeds discarded
- 1 pound ground turkey or beef
- 1 cup cooked rice
- 1 can diced tomatoes
- 1 teaspoon Italian seasoning
- Salt and pepper to taste

### Instructions

1. Preheat oven to 375°F (190°C).
2. In a skillet, brown the meat, then mix in cooked rice, diced tomatoes, Italian seasoning, salt, and pepper.
3. Stuff each bell pepper with the mixture and place them in a baking dish.
4. Cover with foil and bake for 30-35 minutes until peppers are tender.

# Pasta Primavera

## Ingredients

- 8 ounces pasta (penne or rotini)
- 2 cups mixed vegetables (zucchini, bell peppers, carrots, cherry tomatoes)
- 2 cloves garlic, minced
- 1/4 cup olive oil
- Salt and pepper to taste
- Grated Parmesan cheese for serving

## Instructions

1. Cook pasta according to package directions. Drain and set aside.
2. In a skillet, heat olive oil and sauté garlic until fragrant. Add mixed vegetables and cook until tender.
3. Toss cooked pasta with the sautéed vegetables. Season with salt and pepper.
4. Serve topped with grated Parmesan cheese.

## Crispy Fish Tacos

### Ingredients

- 1 pound white fish (cod or tilapia)
- 1 cup breadcrumbs
- 1/2 cup flour
- 2 eggs, beaten
- Corn tortillas
- Toppings: shredded cabbage, salsa, lime wedges

### Instructions

1. Preheat the oven to 400°F (200°C). Line a baking sheet with parchment paper.
2. Dredge fish pieces in flour, dip in egg, then coat with breadcrumbs.
3. Place on the baking sheet and bake for 15-20 minutes until golden and cooked through.
4. Serve in corn tortillas with shredded cabbage and salsa.

# Homemade Lasagna

## Ingredients

- 9 lasagna noodles
- 1 pound ground beef or sausage
- 2 cups ricotta cheese
- 2 cups marinara sauce
- 2 cups shredded mozzarella cheese
- 1/2 cup grated Parmesan cheese
- 1 egg
- Italian seasoning

## Instructions

1. Preheat the oven to 375°F (190°C). Cook lasagna noodles according to package instructions.
2. In a skillet, brown the ground meat. Drain excess fat and mix in marinara sauce.
3. In a bowl, combine ricotta cheese, egg, Italian seasoning, and salt.
4. In a baking dish, layer noodles, ricotta mixture, meat sauce, and mozzarella cheese. Repeat layers, finishing with mozzarella and Parmesan on top.
5. Cover with foil and bake for 25 minutes. Remove foil and bake for an additional 10-15 minutes until cheese is bubbly. Let cool before slicing.

# Grilled Cheese and Tomato Soup

## Ingredients

- 4 slices of bread (white or whole grain)
- 4 slices of cheese (cheddar, American, or your choice)
- 2 tablespoons butter
- 2 cups canned tomato soup
- Salt and pepper to taste

## Instructions

1. In a saucepan, heat tomato soup over medium heat, seasoning with salt and pepper.
2. Butter one side of each slice of bread. Place cheese between two slices (buttered sides out) to make a sandwich.
3. In a skillet, grill the sandwich on medium heat until golden brown and cheese is melted, about 3-4 minutes per side.
4. Serve hot with a bowl of tomato soup.

# Baked Chicken Drumsticks

## Ingredients

- 10 chicken drumsticks
- 2 tablespoons olive oil
- 1 teaspoon garlic powder
- 1 teaspoon paprika
- Salt and pepper to taste

## Instructions

1. Preheat the oven to 425°F (220°C). Line a baking sheet with foil.
2. In a large bowl, toss chicken drumsticks with olive oil, garlic powder, paprika, salt, and pepper until evenly coated.
3. Arrange drumsticks on the baking sheet and bake for 35-40 minutes until cooked through and crispy.
4. Let cool for a few minutes before serving.

## Vegetable Fried Rice

### Ingredients

- 2 cups cooked rice (preferably day-old)
- 1 cup mixed vegetables (peas, carrots, bell peppers)
- 2 eggs, beaten
- 2 tablespoons soy sauce
- 1 tablespoon sesame oil
- 2 green onions, sliced

### Instructions

1. Heat sesame oil in a large skillet or wok over medium-high heat. Add mixed vegetables and sauté until tender.
2. Push vegetables to the side and add beaten eggs, scrambling until cooked.
3. Stir in cooked rice and soy sauce, mixing well. Cook for an additional 3-4 minutes until heated through.
4. Serve hot, garnished with sliced green onions.

# BBQ Pulled Pork Sandwiches

## Ingredients

- 2 pounds pork shoulder
- 1 cup BBQ sauce
- 4 hamburger buns
- Coleslaw (optional for topping)

## Instructions

1. Season pork shoulder with salt and pepper. Cook in a slow cooker on low for 8 hours or until tender.
2. Remove pork and shred it with two forks. Mix with BBQ sauce.
3. Serve the pulled pork on hamburger buns, topped with coleslaw if desired.

# Stuffed Shells with Ricotta

## Ingredients

- 12 jumbo pasta shells
- 1 cup ricotta cheese
- 1 cup marinara sauce
- 1 cup shredded mozzarella cheese
- 1/4 cup grated Parmesan cheese
- 1 egg
- Italian seasoning

## Instructions

1. Preheat the oven to 375°F (190°C). Cook pasta shells according to package directions and drain.
2. In a bowl, mix ricotta cheese, egg, Italian seasoning, and salt.
3. Stuff each shell with the ricotta mixture and place them in a baking dish with marinara sauce on the bottom.
4. Top with remaining marinara sauce and mozzarella cheese. Bake for 25 minutes until cheese is melted and bubbly.

# Coconut Curry Chicken

## Ingredients

- 1 pound chicken breast, cubed
- 1 can coconut milk
- 2 tablespoons red curry paste
- 1 cup mixed vegetables (bell peppers, broccoli)
- 1 tablespoon fish sauce (optional)
- Fresh cilantro for garnish

## Instructions

1. In a skillet, heat a bit of oil over medium heat. Add chicken and cook until browned.
2. Stir in red curry paste and coconut milk, bringing to a simmer.
3. Add mixed vegetables and cook for 10-15 minutes until chicken is cooked through and vegetables are tender.
4. Stir in fish sauce if using and garnish with fresh cilantro before serving.

## Tortilla Wraps with Assorted Fillings

### Ingredients

- 4 large flour or corn tortillas
- Assorted fillings: deli meats, cheese, lettuce, tomatoes, avocado, hummus

### Instructions

1. Lay a tortilla flat and spread a layer of hummus or dressing if desired.
2. Layer your choice of deli meats, cheese, and vegetables on one side of the tortilla.
3. Roll the tortilla tightly, folding in the sides as you go. Cut in half and serve.

# Sweet and Sour Chicken

## Ingredients

- 1 pound chicken breast, cubed
- 1 cup bell peppers, diced
- 1 cup pineapple chunks
- 1/2 cup sweet and sour sauce
- 1 tablespoon cornstarch (optional for thickening)

## Instructions

1. In a skillet, cook chicken over medium heat until browned. Add bell peppers and pineapple, cooking until heated through.
2. Stir in sweet and sour sauce and cook for another 3-5 minutes. If desired, mix cornstarch with a little water and add to the sauce to thicken.
3. Serve hot over rice or noodles.

# Shepherd's Pie

## Ingredients

- 1 pound ground beef or lamb
- 1 onion, diced
- 2 carrots, diced
- 2 cups frozen peas
- 2 tablespoons tomato paste
- 1 cup beef broth
- 4 cups mashed potatoes
- 1 teaspoon Worcestershire sauce
- Salt and pepper to taste
- 1 cup shredded cheddar cheese (optional)

## Instructions

1. Preheat the oven to 400°F (200°C). In a skillet, cook the ground beef with onion and carrots until browned and vegetables are tender.
2. Stir in tomato paste, beef broth, Worcestershire sauce, salt, and pepper. Simmer for 5 minutes.
3. Pour the meat mixture into a baking dish and top with frozen peas. Spread mashed potatoes over the top, smoothing it out.
4. If using, sprinkle cheese on top and bake for 20-25 minutes until golden and bubbling.

# Breakfast-for-Dinner: Pancakes and Sausages

## Ingredients

- 1 cup all-purpose flour
- 2 tablespoons sugar
- 1 tablespoon baking powder
- 1/2 teaspoon salt
- 1 cup milk
- 1 large egg
- 2 tablespoons melted butter
- 6 breakfast sausages

## Instructions

1. In a bowl, mix flour, sugar, baking powder, and salt. In another bowl, whisk together milk, egg, and melted butter.
2. Combine wet and dry ingredients, stirring until just mixed.
3. Heat a griddle or skillet over medium heat. Pour 1/4 cup of batter for each pancake and cook until bubbles form, then flip.
4. Meanwhile, cook sausages according to package instructions. Serve pancakes with syrup and sausages on the side.

**Beef Tacos with All the Fixings**

## Ingredients

- 1 pound ground beef
- 1 packet taco seasoning
- 8 taco shells
- Toppings: shredded lettuce, diced tomatoes, shredded cheese, sour cream, salsa

## Instructions

1. In a skillet, cook ground beef over medium heat until browned. Drain excess fat.
2. Add taco seasoning and according to package instructions.
3. Fill taco shells with seasoned beef and top with your choice of toppings.

# Creamy Tomato Pasta

## Ingredients

- 8 ounces pasta (penne or fusilli)
- 1 can (14 ounces) crushed tomatoes
- 1/2 cup heavy cream
- 2 cloves garlic, minced
- 1 teaspoon Italian seasoning
- Salt and pepper to taste
- Grated Parmesan cheese for serving

## Instructions

1. Cook pasta according to package directions; drain and set aside.
2. In a skillet, heat a bit of oil over medium heat. Sauté garlic until fragrant, then add crushed tomatoes and Italian seasoning.
3. Stir in heavy cream and simmer for 5 minutes. Mix in cooked pasta and toss until combined.
4. Season with salt and pepper. Serve hot, topped with Parmesan cheese.

**Mini Meatloaves**

**Ingredients**

- 1 pound ground beef or turkey
- 1/2 cup breadcrumbs
- 1/2 cup milk
- 1 egg
- 1/4 cup ketchup
- 1 teaspoon garlic powder
- Salt and pepper to taste

**Instructions**

1. Preheat the oven to 350°F (175°C). In a bowl, combine all ingredients until well mixed.
2. Divide the mixture into 8 portions and shape into small loaves on a baking sheet.
3. Bake for 25-30 minutes until cooked through. Serve with additional ketchup if desired.

**Chili Cheese Dogs**

## Ingredients

- 8 hot dogs
- 8 hot dog buns
- 1 can chili (with or without beans)
- 1 cup shredded cheese (cheddar or your choice)

## Instructions

1. Grill or boil hot dogs according to your preference. Warm chili in a saucepan.
2. Place hot dogs in buns and top with warm chili and shredded cheese.
3. Serve immediately, optionally garnished with diced onions or jalapeños.

## Potato and Cheese Pierogi

### Ingredients

- 2 cups mashed potatoes
- 1 cup shredded cheese (cheddar or farmer's cheese)
- 1 package pierogi dough (or make your own)
- 1 onion, diced and sautéed
- Sour cream for serving

### Instructions

1. In a bowl, mix mashed potatoes and cheese until well combined.
2. Roll out pierogi dough and cut into circles. Place a spoonful of potato mixture on each circle, fold, and seal edges.
3. Boil pierogi in salted water until they float, then sauté in a pan with sautéed onion until golden brown.
4. Serve hot with sour cream.

# Vegetable Soup with Grilled Cheese

## Ingredients

- 4 cups vegetable broth
- 2 cups mixed vegetables (carrots, peas, corn)
- 1 onion, diced
- 2 cloves garlic, minced
- 1 can diced tomatoes
- 4 slices bread
- 4 slices cheese (cheddar or American)
- Butter for grilling

## Instructions

1. In a large pot, sauté onion and garlic until softened. Add mixed vegetables and diced tomatoes; cook for 5 minutes.
2. Pour in vegetable broth and simmer for 15-20 minutes. Season with salt and pepper.
3. For grilled cheese, butter one side of each slice of bread. Place cheese between two slices (buttered sides out) and grill in a skillet until golden and cheese is melted.
4. Serve soup hot with grilled cheese on the side.

# Pulled BBQ Chicken Tacos

## Ingredients

- 1 pound boneless, skinless chicken breasts
- 1 cup barbecue sauce
- 8 small tortillas
- Toppings: coleslaw, diced onions, cilantro

## Instructions

1. In a slow cooker, place chicken breasts and cover with barbecue sauce. Cook on low for 6-7 hours or until chicken is tender.
2. Shred the chicken using two forks and mix it with the sauce.
3. Warm tortillas in a skillet or microwave. Fill each tortilla with shredded chicken and top with coleslaw, onions, and cilantro.

# Fish Sticks with Dipping Sauces

## Ingredients

- 1 pound fish fillets (such as cod or haddock)
- 1 cup breadcrumbs
- 1/2 cup flour
- 2 eggs, beaten
- Salt and pepper to taste
- Dipping sauces: tartar sauce, cocktail sauce, or honey mustard

## Instructions

1. Preheat the oven to 400°F (200°C). Cut fish fillets into sticks.
2. Season flour with salt and pepper. Dredge fish sticks in flour, dip in beaten eggs, and coat with breadcrumbs.
3. Place on a baking sheet and bake for 15-20 minutes, turning halfway, until golden brown. Serve with dipping sauces.

# Pasta with Alfredo Sauce

## Ingredients

- 8 ounces fettuccine or pasta of choice
- 1 cup heavy cream
- 1/2 cup grated Parmesan cheese
- 2 tablespoons butter
- 2 cloves garlic, minced
- Salt and pepper to taste

## Instructions

1. Cook pasta according to package instructions; drain and set aside.
2. In a saucepan, melt butter over medium heat and sauté garlic until fragrant. Pour in heavy cream and simmer for 3-5 minutes.
3. Stir in Parmesan cheese until melted and smooth. Season with salt and pepper.
4. Toss cooked pasta with Alfredo sauce and serve hot.

# Chicken and Rice Casserole

## Ingredients

- 2 cups cooked chicken, shredded
- 2 cups cooked rice
- 1 can cream of chicken soup
- 1 cup chicken broth
- 1 cup frozen mixed vegetables
- 1 cup shredded cheese

## Instructions

1. Preheat the oven to 350°F (175°C). In a large bowl, combine chicken, rice, cream of chicken soup, chicken broth, and mixed vegetables.
2. Pour the mixture into a greased casserole dish and top with shredded cheese.
3. Bake for 30-35 minutes until heated through and cheese is melted. Serve warm.

## Baked Potato Bar

### Ingredients

- 4 large baking potatoes
- Toppings: sour cream, shredded cheese, chives, bacon bits, broccoli, butter

### Instructions

1. Preheat the oven to 425°F (220°C). Wash and prick potatoes with a fork.
2. Bake potatoes directly on the oven rack for 45-60 minutes until tender.
3. Once baked, cut a slit in each potato and fluff the insides with a fork. Set up a toppings bar for guests to customize their potatoes.

# Pasta Salad with Veggies and Dressing

## Ingredients

- 8 ounces pasta (bowtie or rotini)
- 1 cup cherry tomatoes, halved
- 1 cucumber, diced
- 1 bell pepper, diced
- 1/2 cup olives, sliced
- 1/2 cup Italian dressing

## Instructions

1. Cook pasta according to package instructions; drain and rinse under cold water.
2. In a large bowl, combine cooked pasta, tomatoes, cucumber, bell pepper, and olives.
3. Drizzle with Italian dressing and toss to coat. Chill in the refrigerator for at least 30 minutes before serving.

# Chicken Enchiladas

## Ingredients

- 2 cups cooked chicken, shredded
- 1 cup enchilada sauce
- 8 corn tortillas
- 1 cup shredded cheese
- Toppings: sour cream, diced green onions

## Instructions

1. Preheat the oven to 350°F (175°C). In a bowl, mix shredded chicken with half of the enchilada sauce.
2. Warm tortillas to make them pliable. Fill each tortilla with chicken mixture, roll, and place in a baking dish seam-side down.
3. Pour remaining enchilada sauce over the top and sprinkle with cheese. Bake for 20-25 minutes until heated through and cheese is bubbly. Serve with sour cream and green onions.

# Tater Tot Casserole

## Ingredients

- 1 pound ground beef
- 1 can cream of mushroom soup
- 1 cup shredded cheese
- 1 bag (32 ounces) tater tots
- 1 cup frozen mixed vegetables (optional)

## Instructions

1. Preheat the oven to 350°F (175°C). In a skillet, brown ground beef until cooked; drain excess fat.
2. In a large bowl, mix cooked beef, cream of mushroom soup, and mixed vegetables if using.
3. Pour mixture into a greased baking dish and top with tater tots. Bake for 30-35 minutes until tater tots are golden brown and crispy.
4. Sprinkle cheese on top in the last 5 minutes of baking. Serve hot.

## Homemade Empanadas

### Ingredients

- 2 cups all-purpose flour
- 1/2 teaspoon salt
- 1/2 cup unsalted butter, chilled and diced
- 1/4 cup cold water
- 1 cup cooked meat (beef, chicken, or cheese)
- 1 egg (for egg wash)

### Instructions

1. In a mixing bowl, combine flour and salt. Cut in butter until the mixture resembles coarse crumbs. Stir in cold water until dough forms a ball.
2. Divide dough into smaller portions and roll each out to about 1/8 inch thick. Cut out circles (about 4-6 inches in diameter).
3. Place a spoonful of the filling in the center of each circle. Fold over and seal edges by pressing with a fork.
4. Preheat oven to 375°F (190°C). Place empanadas on a baking sheet, brush with egg wash, and bake for 20-25 minutes until golden brown.

# Rice and Bean Burritos

## Ingredients

- 1 cup cooked rice
- 1 can black beans, rinsed and drained
- 1 cup shredded cheese
- 4 large flour tortillas
- Salsa, sour cream, and lettuce for serving

## Instructions

1. In a bowl, mix cooked rice, black beans, and shredded cheese. Season with salt and pepper to taste.
2. Place a generous amount of the mixture onto the center of each tortilla. Fold the sides in and roll tightly to enclose the filling.
3. Heat a skillet over medium heat and cook burritos seam-side down until golden brown. Serve with salsa, sour cream, and lettuce.

## Fried Rice with Chicken and Peas

### Ingredients

- 2 cups cooked rice
- 1 cup cooked chicken, diced
- 1/2 cup frozen peas
- 2 eggs, beaten
- 3 tablespoons soy sauce
- 2 green onions, sliced

### Instructions

1. In a large skillet or wok, heat a tablespoon of oil over medium heat. Add beaten eggs and scramble until cooked. Remove from the skillet and set aside.
2. In the same skillet, add more oil if needed and stir-fry the cooked rice, chicken, and peas for 5-7 minutes.
3. Add soy sauce and scrambled eggs, mixing everything together. Cook for an additional 2 minutes. Garnish with sliced green onions and serve hot.

# Minestrone Soup

## Ingredients

- 1 tablespoon olive oil
- 1 onion, diced
- 2 carrots, chopped
- 2 celery stalks, chopped
- 3 garlic cloves, minced
- 1 can diced tomatoes
- 4 cups vegetable broth
- 1 cup green beans, chopped
- 1 cup pasta (small shapes)
- 1 can kidney beans, rinsed and drained
- Italian seasoning, salt, and pepper to taste

## Instructions

1. In a large pot, heat olive oil over medium heat. Add onion, carrots, and celery; sauté until softened.
2. Stir in garlic and cook for 1 minute. Add diced tomatoes, vegetable broth, green beans, and pasta.
3. Bring to a boil, then reduce heat and simmer for about 15 minutes until pasta is tender. Add kidney beans, Italian seasoning, salt, and pepper. Serve hot.

# Teriyaki Chicken with Steamed Broccoli

## Ingredients

- 1 pound chicken breast, sliced
- 1/2 cup teriyaki sauce
- 2 cups broccoli florets
- 2 tablespoons sesame seeds (optional)

## Instructions

1. In a skillet, cook sliced chicken over medium heat until no longer pink, about 5-7 minutes.
2. Pour teriyaki sauce over the chicken, stirring to coat. Cook for an additional 3-4 minutes until the sauce thickens.
3. While chicken is cooking, steam broccoli until tender, about 5 minutes.
4. Serve teriyaki chicken over rice with steamed broccoli on the side. Sprinkle with sesame seeds if desired.

# Egg and Cheese Breakfast Burritos

## Ingredients

- 4 large eggs
- 1/4 cup milk
- 1 cup shredded cheese (cheddar or your choice)
- 4 flour tortillas
- Salt and pepper to taste
- Optional: diced bell peppers, onions, or cooked bacon

## Instructions

1. In a bowl, whisk together the eggs, milk, salt, and pepper. If using, add diced vegetables or cooked bacon.
2. Heat a non-stick skillet over medium heat. Pour in the egg mixture and cook, stirring gently, until the eggs are set but still soft.
3. Place a tortilla on a flat surface, add a portion of the scrambled eggs, and sprinkle with cheese. Roll the tortilla tightly, folding in the sides as you go.
4. Serve warm, with salsa or hot sauce on the side.

## Cheesy Taco Pasta

### Ingredients

- 8 ounces pasta (macaroni or your choice)
- 1 pound ground beef or turkey
- 1 packet taco seasoning
- 1 can diced tomatoes (with green chilies if desired)
- 2 cups shredded cheese (cheddar or Mexican blend)
- 1/2 cup sour cream

### Instructions

1. Cook pasta according to package instructions. Drain and set aside.
2. In a large skillet, brown the ground meat over medium heat. Drain excess fat. Add taco seasoning and diced tomatoes, cooking for another 5 minutes.
3. Stir in cooked pasta and sour cream, mixing until combined. Add cheese and stir until melted. Serve hot.

# Spinach and Cheese Stuffed Shells

## Ingredients

- 12 jumbo pasta shells
- 2 cups ricotta cheese
- 1 cup fresh spinach, chopped
- 1 cup shredded mozzarella cheese
- 1 cup marinara sauce
- 1/4 cup grated Parmesan cheese
- Salt and pepper to taste

## Instructions

1. Preheat the oven to 375°F (190°C). Cook pasta shells according to package directions and drain.
2. In a bowl, combine ricotta cheese, spinach, half of the mozzarella cheese, Parmesan cheese, salt, and pepper.
3. Stuff each cooked shell with the cheese mixture and place in a baking dish. Pour marinara sauce over the shells and sprinkle with remaining mozzarella.
4. Cover with foil and bake for 25 minutes. Remove foil and bake for an additional 10 minutes until cheese is bubbly. Serve hot.

# Beef and Broccoli Stir-Fry

## Ingredients

- 1 pound beef (sirloin or flank steak), thinly sliced
- 2 cups broccoli florets
- 3 tablespoons soy sauce
- 2 tablespoons oyster sauce (optional)
- 1 tablespoon cornstarch
- 2 cloves garlic, minced
- 1 tablespoon vegetable oil

## Instructions

1. In a bowl, marinate the beef with soy sauce, oyster sauce, and cornstarch for about 15 minutes.
2. Heat vegetable oil in a large skillet or wok over high heat. Add garlic and stir-fry for 30 seconds.
3. Add marinated beef and stir-fry until browned. Add broccoli and a splash of water, cooking until broccoli is tender, about 3-5 minutes.
4. Serve hot over rice or noodles.

# Crispy Potato Wedges with Dips

## Ingredients

- 4 large potatoes, cut into wedges
- 3 tablespoons olive oil
- 1 teaspoon garlic powder
- 1 teaspoon paprika
- Salt and pepper to taste
- Optional dips: ranch dressing, ketchup, or aioli

## Instructions

1. Preheat the oven to 425°F (220°C). In a bowl, toss potato wedges with olive oil, garlic powder, paprika, salt, and pepper.
2. Spread wedges in a single layer on a baking sheet. Bake for 30-35 minutes, flipping halfway through, until golden and crispy.
3. Serve hot with your choice of dips.